Healing From Within

Dr. Naumi Munyoki

Dedication

To those on a journey of healing,

This book is dedicated to the silent warriors who battle their inner storms with courage and resilience. To the seekers of peace, the dreamers of wellness, and the believers in the power of self-discovery.

May you find strength in these pages, solace in your solitude, and the wisdom to heal from within.

With heartfelt gratitude for your unwavering spirit and the light you bring to the world.

Acknowledgment

This book would not have been possible without the support, guidance, and inspiration of so many wonderful people in my life.

First and foremost, I want to express my deepest gratitude to my family. Your unwavering love and encouragement have been my anchor. To my parents for their endless patience and for instilling in me the values of perseverance and empathy. To my children Ruth, Diana, and Dennis, whose belief in me never wavered and whose understanding and love have been my greatest source of strength.

A heartfelt thank you to my friends, who listened, supported and cheered me on through every step of this journey. Your companionship has been a beacon of light in times of darkness.

I am profoundly grateful to my mentors and colleagues in the field of healing and wellness. Your wisdom, expertise, and dedication to helping others have inspired me every day.

To my editor and the entire publishing team, thank you for your meticulous attention to detail and for believing in this project. Your hard work and dedication have brought this vision to life.

Finally, to my readers, thank you for allowing me to be a part of your healing journey. I hope this book serves as a source of comfort, insight, and empowerment. Your stories and courage inspire me to continue this work.

About the Author

Naumi Munyoki was born and raised in Kenya, Africa. Her educational journey began at Tanganyika Primary School and continued at Kenya High School in Nairobi. She pursued a Bachelor of Commerce degree from the University of Nairobi and later earned an MBA from Moi University.

In June 2008, Naumi relocated to the United States, where she transitioned into a career in healthcare. She graduated with a Bachelor of Science in Nursing from North Carolina Central University and went on to obtain her Doctor of Nursing Practice (DNP) in Mental Health from the University of North Carolina at Chapel Hill.

Naumi is the founder of Pacific Mind Wellness, an organization dedicated to promoting mental health and wellness. She is a firm believer in evidence-based practice and a holistic approach to care. Her work focuses on anxiety, depression, bipolar disorder, ADHD, and schizophrenia, aiming to provide comprehensive support and healing for her patients.

Preface

Have you ever felt the weight of past experiences holding you back? Perhaps the scars of childhood trauma still linger and continue to color your present, impacting your relationships, your sense of self, your overall well-being, as well as your outlook on life. You are not alone. Millions carry the burdens and scars of past hurts, longing for a path to healing, wholeness, and finding peace and happiness.

This book offers a beacon of hope. Within these pages, you'll discover the transformative power of love and spirituality as strong forces for healing. We'll also explore the impact of trauma on the mind, body, and spirit and will shed light on its various forms and long-term effects. But more importantly, we'll look into the tools and practices that can encourage you to reclaim your life.

But before that, one needs to understand that that journey of healing is not one of erasing the past but of integrating past experiences with a newfound sense of self-compassion and resilience. We'll discover the science behind love's healing power, along with compelling personal stories of individuals who found solace and strength in love's embrace. You'll realize the deep role of spirituality in providing meaning and nurturing connection with the universe and its power.

Throughout this book, we'll be equipping you with practical tools and activities to integrate love and spirituality into your daily life. From cultivating self-love and forgiveness to making healthy connections with others, we'll guide you in building your personalized "healing toolkit." Thus, whether you're just beginning your healing journey or seeking deeper insights, this book is a companion on your path. So, are you ready to set out on your own journey of healing?

Contents

Chapter 1: Introduction

Love and spiritual healing are bound together, creating a powerful combination beyond simple comfort. The ability of love to help us heal is built-in human nature and can effect significant changes on all levels, including spiritual, emotional, and physical.

When the relationship between love and spiritual healing is explored, it becomes clear that when these two energies are beautifully combined, it can result in a path toward wholeness and well-being, a deeper understanding of oneself, and greater interpersonal connections.

In this context, love refers to a universal power that unites people to a common cause, is defined through religious beliefs or a broader feeling of celestial connection, and extends beyond the traditional concept of romantic or familial bonds. Let's understand the concept of spiritual healing and how the power of love can heal us spiritually:

Love as a Healing Power

Love is a transformative and healing energy. It can heal emotional wounds, mend broken hearts, and promote inner calm. A feeling of balance and wholeness enters our lives when we allow the healing energy of love to enter us. Love gives strength when one is weak, comfort when one is hurting, and hope when one is hopeless. It is a spiritual balm that provides us with comfort and rejuvenation.

We become channels for divine energy when we connect with this healing power, deeply transforming and healing others and ourselves. Love can break down boundaries and the false sense of isolation, bringing us to peace and unity. We are all connected by a universal energy existing outside of space and time. The heart's secrets can be unlocked by embodying love in our lives, making it the most potent healing energy and inspiration for spiritual and personal development.

Spiritual Healing

Spiritual healing is an extensive practice that focuses on the mind-body-spirit connection and aims to transform a person's existence. Exploring the person's spiritual aspect and the underlying causes of their distress enhances traditional medical and psychological care. The basic belief is that self-healing involves something greater than oneself. Spiritual healing is a broad term that includes anything from healing with energy and nature-based practices to meditation and prayer. Its core beliefs and intentions can significantly impact the practice's effectiveness, so it's critical to approach it with truthfulness, respect, and a sincere desire to improve.

While spiritual healing has special advantages, it shouldn't be used in place of medical assistance when necessary. This makes integration with traditional care essential. It is crucial to approach professionals or knowledge carefully and ensure it is consistent with one's ethical standards and ideals. In the end, spiritual healing is a very personal path. People can find important tools and insights to assist their growth and well-being by being mindful, approaching it with an open heart, and exercising critical thought.

The power of love can be the most powerful force for spiritual healing, reviving our broken hearts and pushing us forward on the path to wholeness. Here is an in-depth look at the elements that characterize love's transformational power in spiritual healing:

1. Divine and unconditional love:

In spiritual healing, unconditional love is what makes it so special. It's a love that sees past human limits and offers unconditional acceptance and forgiveness.

This affection is often associated with a celestial force believed to originate from a higher power or universal energy. It represents the purest, boundless love.

2. Restoring Emotional wounds:

Love becomes a balm for emotional wounds, offering comfort, understanding, and relief. It provides a secure environment where people can investigate and resolve deep emotional traumas.

A very effective strategy for helping people manage and overcome emotional suffering is the acknowledgment of divine love.

3. Forgiveness and Compassion:

Love helps us let go of negative emotions like hatred and rage by promoting an awareness of the complexities of human nature. Instead of focusing on the past, it encourages openness, growth, acceptance, and non-judgment. This allows us to grow, learn from difficult events, and find peace.

4. Spiritual Purpose and Connection:

The path to spiritual connection is filled with love. It strengthens a person's feeling of purpose and helps them feel more connected to something bigger than themselves.

A guiding factor that gives life purpose and direction is believing in a loving and encouraging greater power.

5. Beyond Separation and Ego:

In spiritual healing, love aids in overcoming self-centered viewpoints and the delusion of separation. It cultivates a feeling of togetherness with all creation, unity, and connectivity.

People get over loneliness and detachment by realizing the divine love that influences everything.

6. Transformational Development:

On a spiritual level, the power of love sparks revolutionary growth. It becomes the force that drives one's development, self-awareness, and consciousness growth.

The transforming power of love can cause massive shifts in an individual's perspective of themselves, others, and the nature of reality.

Both love and spiritual healing have a complex relationship, and each person's experience is different and influenced by their beliefs and practices. Love is cultivated through constant practice and self-reflection.

As a committed mental health specialist, part of my job every day is helping people who are struggling with mental health issues such as depression, anxiety, loneliness, and more. With this book, my goal is to help more people by offering advice on overcoming mental health challenges and dealing with painful childhood traumas. Readers will learn how to identify the effects of traumas on their lives and overall well-being by reading this book.

The main objective is to give people the confidence to admit that they have experienced these traumas, understand their consequences, and start the healing process. This book acts as a guide for individuals facing emotional challenges by accepting the overwhelming prevalence of childhood traumas as key factors to mental health issues. It clarifies the frequently neglected connection between traumatic experiences in the past and present mental health issues.

The book provides helpful and sympathetic recommendations to assist people in overcoming their mental health difficulties, going beyond simple identification. Keeping into consideration the fact that a large number of people with a variety of mental health disorders could find it difficult to pass the trauma test, this book offers insights into the causes of these difficulties, from childhood to adult traumas. Most importantly, this book offers a thorough manual for anyone wishing to recover their mental health and start the process of self-healing. The goal is to give readers the tools and information they need to reflect on themselves and take charge of their mental health.

This book essentially acts as a ray of hope for people who want to manage their mental health issues independently. It seeks to empower readers by providing them with knowledge, direction, and empathy so they may identify, deal with, and eventually move past any traumas that may have impacted their lives.

The effects of trauma can be profoundly psychological, emotional, and physical. Though seeking expert help is necessary, adopting spirituality and compassion can provide beneficial support.

Using Love and Spiritual Healing to Overcome Trauma

At its core, trauma is an extremely intimate and often profound emotion that forever changes a person's emotional and psychological makeup. It is a complex chain of upsetting incidents that overwhelm one's capacity for adjustment and leave enduring effects beyond time. Emotional wounds from trauma can be felt in thoughts, actions, and interpersonal interactions. It is important to understand that there is no "one-size-fits-all" solution or linear path to trauma recovery.

Using spiritual healing and love to overcome trauma can be a compelling process, but you have to approach the process mindfully and with respect for your own journey. The following are some crucial points to consider:

Recognition and Acceptance:

Acknowledging trauma is the first step toward healing, and self-love is essential for accepting incidents without judgment.

Spiritual healing promotes trauma acceptance and connection with a higher force or universal energy, creating the groundwork for understanding life's struggles as part of a greater spiritual journey.

Cultivating Self-Love:

Self-love nurtures kindness, compassion, and understanding, making it a powerful cure for trauma. It promotes self-worthiness, resilience, and a positive self-image. Love for oneself is viewed in spiritual healing as an example of one's relationship to the divine, enabling a more profound realization of one's inner pureness and worth.

Mindfulness and Living in the Present:

Mindfulness and present-moment awareness are essential for healing and navigating trauma. People who are guided by love can grow in self-compassion and patience. A deeper understanding of the relationships of all life is encouraged by mindfulness activities, which are frequently based on spiritual traditions and bring about a sense of peace of mind.

Finding Meaning and Purpose:

Spiritual healing and love are effective means of discovering life's meaning and purpose. While spiritual healing is searching for a greater meaning or purpose, love is the force behind human development and a deeper understanding of life's journeys. A relation with a divine purpose might offer a structure for understanding trauma.

Spiritual Practices for Healing

To heal soulfully and transform their inner self, individuals need to adopt certain practices like:

Mindfulness and Meditation:

These practices can help you become more aware of your thoughts and emotions without judgment. Observing them with detachment lets you gain perspective and learn to manage difficult emotions healthily. Imagine sitting quietly, focusing on your breath, and allowing thoughts and feelings to come and go without getting caught up in them.

Gratitude Practice:

Focusing on the positive aspects of your life, even amidst challenges, can shift your perspective and cultivate resilience. Practice gratitude journaling, expressing appreciation to others, or simply acknowledging the good things in your life. Imagine feeling a sense of thankfulness for the small joys, reminding you of your strength and resilience.

Meaning and Purpose:

Finding meaning in your experiences, even the difficult ones, can be a powerful motivator for healing. Explore your values, passions, and how you can contribute positively to the world. It's like feeling a sense of purpose driving your actions, giving your life meaning beyond the trauma.

Healing trauma is a process rather than a final goal. Embracing spiritual healing and kindness in the process of recovering from trauma is a difficult journey that takes into account every aspect of the human condition. Together, these components offer people perspectives and resources that promote recovery, resiliency, and renewed feelings of purpose and community.

The main theme of this book is using empathy and love to heal. The real meaning of our lives lies within us, in the way we inspire ourselves, raise ourselves above challenging circumstances, and handle ourselves when we're lost.

Through this, you'll acquire a more in-depth understanding of the healing potential of spirituality, love, valuable skills, and knowledge to help you deal with the difficulties associated with trauma recovery. You will learn about your inner power, capacity for forgiveness, and potential to change your life from victim to achiever.

Chapter 2: Understanding Trauma

In its broadest definition, trauma is the emotional reaction to an exceptionally stressful or upsetting experience that exceeds a person's capacity for coping and seriously compromises their sense of security and safety. It may cause long-lasting physical, emotional, and psychological scars on a person. Their sense of security and safety is upset, which makes them feel vulnerable, afraid, and powerless. Even after the traumatic event has occurred, its impact can still be felt, and it influences relationships, ideas, feelings, and behaviors.

It's important to remember that everyone experiences trauma differently, and it also impacts them on different levels. Factors like age, personality, support system, and cultural background influence how people react and cope. Let's dive deep into these factors to better understand the concept of trauma.

Factors Influencing the Impact of Trauma

1. Event Characteristics:

Traumatic events can have various levels of severity, duration, perceived control, and type. Events that pose a greater risk to life, such as violent attacks or natural disasters, are given more weight than insignificant mishaps. Extended periods of trauma exposure, such as ongoing abuse or neglect, may disrupt coping strategies and result in more profound emotional and psychological wounds. Fear and anxiety might worsen after a distressing event if one feels helpless and powerless.

Furthermore, interpersonal violence and betrayal by a trusted figure are two examples of trauma types that can be very harmful because they go against fundamental beliefs about safety and trust, which makes the healing process even more difficult.

2. Personal Characteristics:

Children's lack of maturity in terms of both mental and emotional abilities makes them prone to the long-term detrimental effects of traumatic experiences, especially the younger ones. Strong personality traits like resilience and optimism can buffer against trauma, but pre-existing mental health disorders can amplify its effects.

People who possess constructive coping mechanisms, such as problem-solving, social support, and mindfulness, are far better at handling difficult emotions. While isolation can worsen the effects, a strong social support network, such as friends, family, or therapists, can offer a safe space for healing.

3. Cultural Factors:

Cultures that have different views on trauma—some that encourage free communication while others repress feelings can have an impact on how people understand and communicate their experiences. Understanding these conventions is essential to offering culturally sensitive support. The stigma associated with some forms of trauma may interfere with healing and affect behaviors related to seeking assistance.

The recovery process also benefits greatly from the involvement of community resources, including support groups, therapists, and conventional treatment methods. Those with limited resources may find it difficult to locate culturally appropriate forms of assistance.

4. Socioeconomic Factors:

Discrimination and poverty can intensify coping mechanisms for trauma, making it more difficult to acquire necessary services like therapy and medical treatment. Systemic inequalities intensify additional stresses that marginalized people frequently encounter, such as racism, sexism, and homophobia. Unfair access to healthcare, in particular to mental health services, can pose serious barriers to treatment, particularly for communities that are marginalized, making the healing process even more difficult. Resolving these problems is essential to post-traumatic healing.

While some people may suffer severe negative effects, others may emerge stronger and more resilient from the situation. The most important lesson is that trauma has a distinct and complicated effect, and by learning all of these components, we may better assist people in their healing processes. Moving forward, let's explore the different types of trauma people may encounter.

Types of Traumas

Trauma is the body's reaction to upsetting experiences, leading to a variety of short- and long-term feelings. According to a World Health Organization (WHO) report, trauma affects at least one-third of people at some point. Pain, loss, betrayal, misuse of authority, powerlessness, and disorientation are common aftereffects of trauma. These are some of the most common types of traumas that experts have classified:

1. Secondary Trauma:

It differs from other forms of trauma in that people experience trauma in this instance when they talk to or hear from someone who has personally experienced trauma.

People who are listening may occasionally soak up upsetting details of the traumatic experience, which could harm their mental health.

2. Incidental Trauma:

This type of trauma is the long-term effects of an upsetting incident, like an accident, abuse, or natural disaster, which can hurt a person physically and emotionally and change their behavior. Panic, anxiety, disorientation, annoyance, poor sleep patterns, loss of attention, and distrust of people are typical symptoms.

3. Complex Trauma:

A complex trauma can have a variety of impacts, including violence, abuse, and problems in the family. People who have experienced significant trauma frequently go into survival mode, adopt a pessimistic mindset, and acquire "Mean World Syndrome." They feel misinterpreted by people around them and suffer from emotional overload.

These types can worsen into more diverse and problematic mental health problems if not taken care of properly. But one type that is considered to be the most prominent cause of trauma is developmental trauma, or we can simply say childhood trauma.

4. Childhood Trauma:

One major kind of trauma is developmental trauma, which is caused by unfavorable childhood experiences like physical, sexual, or emotional abuse, abandonment, rejection, betrayal, or even death. It disturbs a child's identity and hinders wholesome connections. Developmental trauma survivors are more likely to experience mental health issues, including post-traumatic stress disorder (PTSD). Children are especially at risk for trauma because of the way their developing brains release stress and fear-related hormones. A child's brain development is disturbed by developmental trauma, which can have long-term consequences.

Adverse Childhood Trauma (ACEs) and Its Dangers

Adverse childhood experiences, or ACEs, are another name for childhood trauma. They are frightening incidents that can result in violent, hazardous, or tragic situations. An estimated 46% of kids experience it at some point in their lives. Despite the resilience of children, people tend to forget about childhood trauma since they may not recall it as an adult. However, recognizing that childhood trauma can have long-lasting effects is essential as it dictates most of our behaviors as adults. [1]

---

[1] https://www.samhsa.gov/sites/default/files/brief_report_natl_childrens_mh_aw areness_day.pdf

A child may have experienced trauma from physical or sexual abuse, a single traumatic event (such as a car accident or natural disaster), the death of a loved one, or a serious medical event. Traumatic events can also result from ongoing stress, such as being bullied or living in a dangerous neighborhood. Childhood trauma doesn't need to result from direct experiences, such as seeing a loved one struggle with a serious illness or being exposed to violent media, which can be extremely disturbing for them.

The Kaiser Permanente Adverse Childhood Experiences (ACEs) Study, which ran from 1995 to 1997, is a noteworthy study that looked into how childhood maltreatment and neglect affect people's health and well-being in later life. More than 17,000 people answered private questionnaires regarding their activities, health, and early experiences.[2]

Researchers looked at how these ten ACEs related to one another:

- Physical abuse of children

- Sexual abuse of children

- Emotional abuse of children

- Neglecting emotions

- Physical disregard

- An individual suffering from mental illness, depression, or suicidal thoughts at home, Addict or alcoholic family member

---

[2]https://eclkc.ohs.acf.hhs.gov/publication/trauma-adverse-childhood-experiences-aces

- Observing the mother being victimized by spousal abuse

- Losing a parent due to their divorce or passing away

- Any family member imprisoned for a criminal offense

According to the ACE study, a person's health results in later life are greatly impacted by their traumatic events. Stress triggers the body's physiologic release of cortisol, which can result in toxic stress and impair the brain's ability to learn. Traumatized students are more likely to struggle in the classroom and experience academic failure.

These days, childhood trauma is a major issue. Its symptoms are typically ignored, yet they brutally murder a person from the inside out. It possesses some of the worst impacts on a person, and if ignored, the ramifications will last a lifetime.

Adverse Effects of Childhood Trauma

When a child experiences trauma during childhood, it can overwhelm their coping mechanisms and have a lasting effect on every aspect of their life. These are some of them.

Physical Impact:

Children who have experienced trauma may not reach their full potential and experience delays in their immune system, physical development, and central nervous system growth. According to a 2015 study, there is a link between repeated trauma and an increased chance of developing chronic illnesses like diabetes, asthma, heart disease, and stroke. A further examination of 134 research-based publications published in 2019 emphasizes the chance of growing older and experiencing higher degrees of pain as well as illnesses like cancer, lung disease, cardiovascular disease, and autoimmune diseases. [3]

Impact on Mental Health:

Childhood trauma can have a serious negative effect on mental health, increasing the risk of PTSD, psychotic illnesses, depression, emotional distress, high-stress levels, and problems controlling aggressive behavior. When individuals are subjected to complicated traumas, they may cognitively dissociate themselves from the event. Studies reveal that adults who grew up with parental domestic violence, sexual abuse, or physical abuse are more likely to attempt suicide later in life. This emphasizes how critical it is for mental health professionals to comprehend and treat childhood trauma. [4]

Social Life and Relationships:

Adverse childhood trauma can result in challenges in the workplace and classroom, trouble establishing and sustaining good relationships, and an elevated risk of victimization. Healthy connections with family, friends, and love partners can be affected by trust issues, emotional dysregulation, and intimacy fear. Victims might not have the knowledge or abilities to stay clear of dangerous situations.

Furthermore, emotional and cognitive impacts can reduce chances for professional success and hinder academic

---

[3]https://www.tandfonline.com/doi/full/10.1080/2331205X.2019.1581447
[4]https://www.psychiatrictimes.com/view/effects-childhood-trauma-depression-and-suicidality-adulthood

achievement. It might be difficult to establish positive relationships with people in positions of authority.

Generational Cycle:

People who have gone through traumatic experiences as children may find it difficult to learn positive parenting techniques, which could put their own kids at risk of going through similar experiences. This starts an alarming cycle of pain across generations that needs to be broken by deliberate action.

Trauma leaves scars on your body, mind, and spirit, which makes you feel like disassociating yourself from this world and the people in your life. With the right resources, support, and early intervention, childhood trauma can be treated. Establishing a strong network of support and gaining expert assistance are essential measures. Creating a safe environment for kids and promoting preventive measures can reduce the likelihood of trauma and its long-term effects.

Impact of Trauma on the Mind, Body, and Spirit

Childhood or adulthood trauma can have a significant and long-lasting effect on the mind, body, and spirit. It's crucial to keep in mind that the impacts are different and highly dependent on the person, the kind of trauma, and the accessibility of resources. Here's a broad summary of how trauma might impact each of these areas, though:

Mind:

Emotional distress, cognitive challenges, negative thought habits, and dissociation can all result from traumatic experiences. These can lead to intense emotions such as terror, wrath, guilt, sadness, anxiety, and worry that can interfere with day-to-day activities and have an impact on relationships, employment, and education. Dissociation may also be used as a coping strategy to lessen the trauma's suffering.

Body:

Trauma can result in weaker immune systems, persistent pain, headaches, stomachaches, exhaustion, and sleep difficulties, among other physical symptoms. Changes in sleeping and eating routines can result in unhealthy patterns and raise the possibility of substance misuse. Extreme vigilance can also be draining and detrimental to day-to-day functioning.

Spirit:

Trauma can have a significant effect on our soul, leading us to doubt our identity and mission. Moreover, it might undermine trust, which makes it challenging to connect with people or with ourselves. A person can get hopelessly consumed, which diminishes optimism and faith in a better future. Some individuals may disconnect from their spiritual beliefs or practices as a way to cope with the pain.

These are only a few of the possible effects; not everyone will be affected in every way. The most important lesson is that trauma impacts a person's entire being, not just one part. It takes care of all these connected pieces to heal.

The brain's healing capacity is remarkable. People can recover from trauma and regain their sense of safety and well-being with the right support and therapy. In addition to self-compassion and kindness being necessary for resilience building and conquering trauma-related challenges, a network of supporting family, friends, and therapists is important for the healing process.

Common Coping Mechanisms from Trauma

People cope with trauma in many different ways, and what works for one person may not work for another. Some coping mechanisms are healthy, but some are unhealthy approaches that will not help for long-term well-being but cause emotional damage to yourself. A few common coping techniques include:

Healthy Coping Techniques

Problem Focused:

Trauma can be managed by asking for help from family and friends, seeing a professional, addressing the underlying reason, practicing deep breathing and meditation, and partaking in hobbies and physical activity that promote health. These techniques can aid in stress reduction, promote serenity, and enhance general well-being.

Emotion Focused:

It can be therapeutic to process and let go of negative feelings when trauma experiences are shared in a secure setting. Self-awareness and emotional control are enhanced by practicing mindfulness and self-compassion. Writing, music, and other creative endeavors can be therapeutic and relieving. Healthy humor can connect and find lightheartedness, but it should not minimize trauma itself.

Meaning Focused:

Accepting difficult situations can empower people and promote growth. Making a spiritual or religious connection can offer support and direction when things are tough. People can overcome obstacles in the future and gain value from their past experiences by focusing on personal growth and resilience.

Unhealthy Coping Techniques

They may offer temporary relief, but ultimately, they hinder healing and can cause further harm. Here's a breakdown of why they're problematic:

Avoidance:

Processing trauma won't happen if thoughts and feelings are overlooked or ignored, which can result in emotional buildup and destructive expressions. Loneliness and isolation can be triggered by being alone, which makes it more difficult to get help and develop strength. Stay clear of trauma triggers to avoid exposure and desensitization, which may slow down the healing process.

Substance use:

Addiction to alcohol, drugs, or other substances may worsen the underlying trauma and lead to addiction, health issues, and temporary numbness.

Self-harm:

Causing physical or emotional harm to oneself is a risky and destructive coping mechanism that can result in severe wounds, heightened emotional pain, or even suicide.

There are many effective and healthy ways to cope with trauma, and seeking professional support can help someone who's seeking help to cure their traumas and sorrows. It's crucial to understand the limitations of coping mechanisms so people can make informed choices about how to manage their trauma and seek appropriate support.

Limitations of Coping Mechanisms

Here's a more detailed breakdown of each limitation:

1. Uniqueness: What works for one person might not work for another due to individual differences in personalities, experiences, and trauma severity.

2. Temporal Dependence: Effectiveness can vary over time. A mechanism that provides relief initially might become ineffective or even harmful later as the trauma processing deepens.

3. Avoidance of Root Cause: Some coping mechanisms might mask the underlying trauma and prevent individuals from confronting and healing the core issues.

4. Symptom Specificity: Not every symptom is treated by every mechanism. Some, for instance, may successfully numb emotional suffering but not unwanted memories. Combining several strategies is typically necessary to address a range of symptoms.

5. Potential for Harm: Unhealthy coping mechanisms like avoidance, substance use, or self-harm can offer temporary relief but ultimately cause more harm and hinder healing.

Consulting with therapists or counselors can offer customized approaches and assistance in overcoming obstacles in the recovery process. For thorough recovery, a balanced strategy that combines problem-focused, emotion-focused, and meaning-focused coping techniques is advised.

Coping skills may need to change as healing is a dynamic process. In case you are unable to establish healthy coping techniques on your own or feel trapped, you must seek expert assistance. Professionals with the necessary qualifications can help you on your path to recovery and well-being.

Understanding trauma is a complex process that involves acknowledging its profound impact on our lives and not putting blame. Healing from trauma is a journey that can be challenging, but it's essential to remember that you are not alone. By shifting the perspective from a victim to a survivor, you can regain control of your life, build resilience, and live a life with purpose. You can overcome trauma and come out stronger and more confident with help and understanding.

Chapter 3: Love and Spirituality

Love is a complex and versatile emotion. It is frequently described as a powerful and good emotion that includes feelings of affection, compassion, warmth, and happiness. It can take many forms, from romantic love's passionate intensity to familial love's comforting stability.

Love often involves a deep emotional attachment to another person or thing. This attachment can be based on shared experiences, values, or a sense of connection. It creates a desire for closeness and a willingness to invest in the well-being of the loved one. It is a sense of commitment, whether it is the dedication to raising a kid, the loyalty shared between friends, or the promise of marriage. This commitment entails putting the well-being of the loved one first and making sacrifices for their sake.

The feeling of love promotes the desire to do good for the loved ones. This can be reflected in actions of kindness, support, and understanding. In some instances, you must prioritize the needs and happiness of a loved one over your own.

It is a tremendous motivator for personal development. It can motivate us to become better versions of ourselves by pushing us out of our comfort zones and motivating us to learn new skills and attributes.

Love is not a singular expression. It comes in different forms, and everyone has their unique way of showing and receiving it. Numerous philosophical theories on love explore its nature, origins, and significance. Some prominent theories focus on love as a divine force, a social construct, or a biological drive. Different cultures have different understandings and expressions of love. What constitutes acceptable or desirable forms of love can vary greatly across societies. Ultimately, the definition of love is shaped by individual experiences and interpretations. Each person may have a unique understanding of what love means to them.[5]

The Different Types of Love

Here's a deeper look into the forms of love, the way people perceive them, and how it impacts our lives as well:

1. Self-Love:

What you have is what you give. How true is it that if you don't have love for yourself, how can you give it to others? This is what self-love is. Before loving someone, it is necessary to first build that feeling for yourself.

Many people often overlook the importance of self-love, but having that feeling in your heart and your soul works wonders for you. It involves valuing our worth, respecting our needs and boundaries, and caring for our physical and mental well-being. Self-love is basically the love and acceptance we have for ourselves.

Self-care and well-being involve realizing our basic worth, recognizing our needs and limits, and caring for our bodily and mental health. This includes giving our bodies nutritious foods, participating in enjoyable activities, and getting expert support

---

[5]https://www.verywellmind.com/what-is-love-2795343

when necessary. Self-love is essential for developing good relationships with others based on mutual respect and understanding.

2. Romantic Love:

This is one of the most common kinds of love. Romantic love is passionate and intense and requires profound affection, intimacy, desire, and devotion. It involves more than just physical attraction; it also requires emotional openness, trust, and understanding. Sexual attraction and physical intimacy are crucial components, as is a genuine desire for long-term relationships. However, it comes with its challenges; jealousy and conflicts are on top of them. Intimacy and commitment lead to jealousy, whereas differences in needs, attitudes, and communication styles cause conflict. It is important to balance individual needs and relational demands.

Romantic love varies by culture and individual, with definitions ranging according to personal ideals and customs. It can be long-term or temporary, and its expression can change with time from intense passion to deeper, more companionate love.

3. Platonic Love:

This deep and meaningful love exists between friends or family members without any romantic or sexual desire. It's based on shared values, mutual respect, trust, and understanding. Platonic love provides companionship, support, and a sense of belonging and can be just as important as romantic love in our lives.

It creates a safe space for people to seek emotional support to people so they can share their pleasures and vulnerabilities without being judged. The type of unconditional love and acceptance it raises increases self-esteem and worth. It helps build lifelong companionship, creating a reliable bond between two people. They share ideas and experiences that lead to personal progress, and fun and laughter generate long-term memories.

Navigating platonic love requires keeping open communication, respecting individual needs and space, acknowledging achievements, and offering support during difficult times. Handling romantic feelings openly is critical to maintaining friendships and healthy relationships.

Love comes in many forms and is a healing source for many people. The love we have for people and the love we give them heal most of the parts of our souls. That's the reason why we are mostly afraid of losing them; it aches our souls. Let's look deeper into how spirituality heals people and what its impacts are.

Spirituality and Its Role in Healing

Spirituality is a broad concept that encompasses a person's search for meaning, purpose, and connection to something more than oneself. This can include religious views, but it can also refer to larger philosophical and existential issues and a connection to nature or the universe.

For many people, spirituality provides comfort and release from stress. Research indicates that individuals who use religion to deal with life's challenges benefit from several health and well-being benefits.[6]

Spirituality does not refer to a specific path or belief system. There are numerous ways to engage in spirituality and gain its advantages. Spirituality is defined differently by each individual. Some people believe in a higher power or follow a certain religious practice. Others may describe it as feeling linked to a higher state or interconnected with the rest of humanity and nature. However, spirituality will ultimately heal a person no matter in which form, but it does.

How can spirituality aid healing?

Coping: Spiritual beliefs and practices can bring peace, strength, and hope in the face of illness or hardship. This can help people deal with stress, anxiety, and sadness, resulting in better mental and emotional well-being.

Meaning-making: Sickness might cause profound reflections about life, death, and suffering. Spirituality can provide a framework for understanding and finding meaning in these experiences, which is essential for healing.

Social support: Many spiritual communities offer social support and connections, which benefit overall health and well-being. They can provide a sense of community, acceptance, and practical aid during difficult times.

Mind-body practices: Many spiritual traditions include meditation, prayer, yoga, and mindfulness, which are proven to

---

[6] https://pubmed.ncbi.nlm.nih.gov/29892314/

provide various health benefits, such as stress reduction, increased sleep, and pain relief.

While precise spiritual beliefs are a matter of faith, research has established some advantages of spirituality and spiritual activities. The findings may not surprise anyone who has found solace in their religious or spiritual beliefs. Still, they are remarkable because they show scientifically that these activities help a large number of people. One study shows that religion and spirituality can help people cope with the effects of daily stress. One study discovered that everyday spiritual experiences helped older persons better cope with negative moods and increased positive feelings.[7]

Spirituality and prayer are helpful stress management strategies for both young and old people. According to research, prayer and spirituality improve health and psychological well-being, reduce depression and hypertension, increase pleasant moods, and improve stress management.[8]

How to Practice Spirituality?

The beauty of spirituality lies in its personal nature. While everyone's path is different, here are some practical actions and tools to help you start your exploration and improve your well-being:

---

[7]https://academic.oup.com/psychsocgerontology/article/67/4/456/567333
[8]https://link.springer.com/article/10.1007/s10943-018-0564-8

Inner Exploration:

Mindfulness is the discipline of paying attention to feelings and events without judgment, which can be developed through activities such as meditation, journaling, or being outside. Self-reflection involves setting aside silent reflection while asking questions about values, meaning, purpose, joy, and grief. Journaling is an effective way to reflect and process ideas. Both activities encourage increased consciousness and self-awareness.

Connecting with Others:

Getting involved in volunteering allows you to connect with greater concerns and develop compassion. Find a cause you are passionate about and devote time to volunteering. Join a community with similar spiritual interests, such as a religious community, meditation group, or book club, to share your journey and find support and inspiration.

Cultivating Practices:

Meditation is an ancient practice that offers stress relief, self-awareness, and inner calm. It can be performed daily with guided meditations or simple breathing exercises. Expressing gratitude is a daily practice that can be kept in a gratitude diary or shared with others. Yoga, which combines physical postures, breathing exercises, and mindfulness, can increase flexibility, reduce stress, and promote general well-being. These practices help heal more efficiently and bring you peace and comfort.

Resources and Inspiration:

It can be helpful to search for alternatives that can be the simplest yet most effective resource for oneself in spiritual recovery. Explore spiritual writings, listen to podcasts and lectures, and attend seminars and retreats to understand spirituality better. Engage in different conversations about meditation, yoga, and natural connection.[9]

The relationship between spirituality and healing is complex and fascinating, with a long history and diverse perspectives. While it's important to remember that spirituality is not a replacement for medical treatment, it can significantly affect the healing process on multiple levels.

The Symbiotic Relationship Between Love and Spirituality

Love and spirituality are deeply interconnected concepts that share a profound symbiotic relationship as vast as the universe. Here are some reflections on this profound connection:

Love as the Foundation of Spirituality:

Many spiritual traditions value unconditional love as a reflection of the divine or a means of spiritual growth. By promoting love for oneself, others, and the world around us, we gain access to a higher reality beyond our identities.

Spirituality frequently aims to connect us to something greater than ourselves, whether it be a higher power, nature, or mankind in general. Love serves as a bridge that helps us to make

---

[9]https://www.verywellmind.com/how-spirituality-can-benefit-mental-and-physical-health-3144807#citation-7

these relationships, instilling a sense of belonging and oneness. True love, in its purest form, transforms us. It opens our hearts, challenges our preconceptions, and motivates us to be better versions of ourselves. This is consistent with the basic purpose of many spiritual approaches: promoting human growth and inner transformation.

Spirituality Deepening Love:

Spirituality can expand our capacity for love beyond romantic relationships by encouraging compassion, empathy, and forgiveness for all. It offers a framework for understanding love, guiding us through complex emotions, and cultivating healthy relationships. Spiritual teachings provide insights into the nature of love, its problems, and its ultimate purpose, which improves our awareness of its depth and strength. Connecting love to a larger spiritual context can give our acts greater meaning and purpose, inspiring us to express love more truly and totally.

The Symbiotic Cycle:

Love and spirituality have a reciprocal relationship. It's a lovely dance in which one supports the other, resulting in a positive feedback cycle. As we nurture love, we open ourselves up to spiritual experiences, and as our spirituality grows, so does our capacity for love.

Eventually, this symbiotic relationship can lead to a more satisfying and meaningful life. It enables us to connect deeply and authentically with ourselves, others, and the world around us, enriching our journeys while also contributing to a more loving and caring world.

Spirituality inspires people to pursue love daily through simple acts of kindness or larger partnerships. This approach offers delight and improves one's life. It teaches us to embrace all forms of love and to honor everyone who gives. Spirituality promotes greater love and relationships by encouraging acceptance and the chance to meet someone looking for one.

Chapter 4: Love as a Healing Force

'Love cures people - both the ones who give it and the ones who receive it,' claimed psychiatrist Karl Menninger.[10] When we feel miserable, we seek our loved ones because we crave that feeling that soothes our disturbed thoughts. Love heals us spiritually and helps us grow better in our lives.

Love is a fleeting emotion that must be cherished at all times. While you love someone, you may not always feel completely connected to that emotion. Sometimes, you behave out of anger rather than love, but reconnecting with loving feelings can help you reproach issues with care. Love is like an underground river that must be discovered for nourishment.

However, the "healing power of love" is a topic investigated by both science and psychology, with differing methods and levels of evidence. Here's the breakdown of each perspective:

Scientific Perspective

While research doesn't definitively prove a direct cause-and-effect link between love and physical healing, studies suggest correlations. For example, social support (often associated with love) has been linked to:

---

[10]https://www.ncbi.nlm.nih.gov/pmc/articles/PMC8605763/

Faster recovery from illness:

According to studies, people with great social support recover from surgery faster and less discomfort.[11]

Improved immunological function:

Love and social connection may strengthen the immune system, thus aiding in the battle against illnesses.

Reduced stress:

Supportive relationships can act as a stress buffer, which has been linked to medical illnesses.

Some researchers explore potential biological pathways linking love to health. For example, oxytocin, often called the "love hormone," might play a role in reducing stress hormones and promoting healing. However, these mechanisms are still under investigation.

Psychological Perspective

According to research, love has a major impact on mental and emotional well-being. It reduces stress and anxiety, improves physical health, provides a sense of stability and belonging, encourages good emotions such as joy and appreciation, and strengthens coping skills. These advantages are related to the emotional and psychological resources offered by supportive

---

[11] https://pubmed.ncbi.nlm.nih.gov/34108418/

relationships, which can help individuals deal with difficulties and improve their mental health.[12]

Many people struggle with mental health and want to find ways in which to cope with their thoughts, feelings, and emotions healthily. The constant love and support of family and friends can frequently help them to heal from trauma or loss. Moreover, romantic love in their lives promotes resilience and growth, which connects them emotionally and helps them work toward common goals. Self-love is an effective healing force that includes self-discovery, forgiveness, and healthy self-esteem.

Here are some stories of people who emphasize the importance of shared experiences, emotional affirmation, and practical support in recovery.

Finding Healing in Self-Love: Roxane Gay's Journey in "Hunger"

Roxane Gay's memoir "Hunger" is a fascinating investigation of pain, recovery, and our complicated relationship with our bodies. Gay describes her abusive background, which left her disconnected from her body and terrified of being judged in honest admissions. Her story is full of internalized negativity and pain. However, "Hunger" is a story of resistance rather than despair. Gay starts on a journey of self-discovery, challenging social beauty standards and negative prejudices.

Despite the difficulties, she finds peace in writing, helpful connections, and her vital worth of herself. The memoir

---

[12]https://brilliantio.com/why-love-
matters/#:~:text=When%20you%E2%80%99re%20in%20a%20loving%20relationship%2
C%20you%E2%80%99re%20likely,love%20boosts%20your%20overall%20mental%20hea
lth%20and%20well-being.

acknowledges the messy nature of recovery while also celebrating the accomplishments, such as Gay's acceptance of her scars as a powerful act of reclaiming her body and story.

The story concludes with a subtle revolution in which Gay accepts her body as a means of experience and a source of strength. "Hunger" is a global song for anybody who has struggled with self-doubt and body image concerns, reminding us that healing is not a linear process and that self-love is a journey rather than a destination.

From War Trauma to Family Love: Ishmael Beah's Journey in "A Long Way Home"

"A Long Way Home" is a memoir by Ishmael Beah, a former child soldier who was compelled to join a rebel army during Sierra Leone's civil war. The story depicts the savagery of war and the enduring power of love and family in the face of terrible trauma. The war wrecks Beah's youth, but he finds comfort in his foster parents, Merron and Laura, who provide unconditional love, compassion, and understanding. They establish an environment in which he can recover and communicate his grief and fear without being judged.

The path to recovery is difficult, but with each shared meal, meaningful conversation, and acceptance, Beah moves forward. He finds refuge in writing, translating his experiences into art, and reconnecting with his education.

"A Long Way Home" acknowledges the scars conflict creates while celebrating the human spirit's endurance. It demonstrates how love, compassion, and a stable atmosphere may provide fruitful ground for healing and growth. Beah's story goes beyond his personal experience and becomes a global message of hope for anybody experiencing tragedy, loss, or displacement.

Love has healing powers, and it continues to prove to us that without this feeling, our lives would become a depressed place. Several case studies have been taken to make it clear that we should practice actions that show love and empathy.

Healing Through Love: Case Studies

Here are some case studies showcasing the healing power of love in various contexts:

Love of Nature Heals Addiction:

A case study was done of a man who suffered years from addiction. He was isolated and hopeless and didn't know how to cure it.

After some time, he found this organization where people volunteer to help others. He found comfort in volunteering for an environmental organization, reconnecting with nature, and finding meaning in helping others. The organization's emphasis on environment and community gave him a support structure and a reason to conquer his addiction.

The love for nature offered a sense of belonging, purpose, and responsibility, contributing to the man's recovery from addiction.

Love of Learning Heals Refugee Youth

Young refugees faced trauma, displacement, and limited educational opportunities. A community center offered them access to education and extracurricular activities, fostering a sense of normalcy and hope. The love for learning and the supportive environment helped them overcome challenges, develop skills, and build a brighter future.

The love for learning provided a safe space for development, hope, and empowerment, contributing to the well-being and prospects of the refugee youth.

These are just a few examples; love and healing can take many different forms. Love can appear in a variety of forms, including self-love, familial love, romantic love, community love, and love for a cause, all of which contribute to healing in different circumstances.

The Healing Power of Empathy, Compassion, and Connection

Empathy, compassion, and connection are more than just pleasant feelings; they are powerful forces that play an important part in the healing process, both individually and collectively.

Empathy:

Empathy is described as the ability to feel and comprehend the experiences of others. Basically, it is the ability to put oneself in the shoes of another. It is a learned habit, yet some people are born with a greater ability to empathize. A sense of empathy means viewing the world through another person's eyes, allowing us to acknowledge and validate their emotions and experiences. This shift in viewpoint creates compassion and a deeper concern for their well-being, encouraging us to provide support and encouragement, establishing a safe healing space.

Compassion:

Empathy is putting yourself in the shoes of others and experiencing their sorrow, but compassion requires a sincere desire or act to ease another's suffering and to be with them in their suffering.

Compassion is a strong tool that inspires empathy and action, allowing people to enhance their well-being through practical assistance, emotional consolation, or a listening ear. It also helps the provider connect with their humanity and establish a sense of purpose, contributing to their well-being by observing others' suffering.

Connection:

Connectivity is essential to healing, providing a sense of security, affirmation, and belonging. It can help reduce stress, improve mental well-being, and boost healing motivation. Making connections necessitates honesty, vulnerability, and actively seeking out helpful communities.

Participating in common activities, showing thanks, and providing genuine support might help to strengthen these bonds. Sharing experiences helps normalize the healing process, lessen feelings of loneliness, and provide vital insights and suggestions. Connecting with individuals who share similar experiences might help you handle challenging situations or emotions.

Sharing experiences with others and learning theirs promotes a sense of community and belonging, which helps people feel less alone and more supported on their healing journey.

The Healing Power of Empathy to Recover Childhood Trauma

Childhood trauma can have severe and long-term consequences for an individual's emotional, psychological, and physical well-being. However, the power of empathy, compassion, and connection can help tremendously with the healing process.

Empathy is a vital tool for survivors to comprehend better their pain, emotions, and the consequences of trauma. It promotes a sense of validation and belonging by actively listening, acknowledging emotions, and avoiding judgment. Empathy also helps interrupt the cycle of isolation by creating a secure space in which the survivor feels heard and understood, lowering their loneliness.

Compassion goes beyond comprehension, expressing true care and concern for individuals. It makes them feel supported and free of judgment. Witnessing compassion can help you develop self-compassion, which is an essential element of healing. This is treating oneself with kindness and empathy while challenging negative self-beliefs and shame that are frequently associated with trauma.

Trauma can undermine trust, making it difficult to build healthy relationships. Establishing safe and supportive relationships with therapists, family, friends, or support groups can help you feel more connected and secure. Sharing trauma experiences in a safe environment can be therapeutic, promoting understanding and shared strength while minimizing feelings of isolation and shame.

Love and kindness create a healing environment. Empathy lowers stress and terror, boosts self-esteem, and empowers survivors. It reduces stress hormones and anxiety, increases resilience, and allows people to take control of their healing process. This aids in recovery and gives hope for a better future.

Love is not a magic cure, and the specific ways it promotes healing can vary depending on individual needs and circumstances. Cultivating this feeling in your life, for yourself and others, can significantly enhance your well-being and create a more supportive and healing environment for yourself and those around you.

Chapter 5: Spiritual Pathways to Healing

"Human beings, by changing the inner attitudes of their minds, can change the outer aspects of their lives."

-William James

Facing a life-threatening or chronic illness is often a life-altering experience. Many people find their lives turned upside down, no longer able to work, and struggling to manage daily activities due to constant appointments and therapies. This overwhelming situation can push them to seek alternative ways to cope and find meaning beyond the limitations imposed by their illness.

Thankfully, research suggests that non-traditional approaches, such as emotional support, meditation, visualization, spirituality, and positive self-talk, can play a significant role in the healing journey. These practices can offer valuable tools to navigate the emotional and spiritual challenges accompanying a health crisis and contribute to a more holistic approach to well-being.

A Journey of Discovery: Exploring Different Spiritual Paths

The human desire for purpose and connection frequently takes us on a journey that includes spiritual discovery. Many people find comfort, growth, and happiness in various practices, each offering a special way to establish a connection with something greater than themselves. Here is a quick overview of a few popular spiritual practices:

1. Meditation: A Stillness within the Storm

This practice involves training the mind to achieve a state of focused awareness and inner calm. Meditators aim to quiet the mind's constant chatter and cultivate a sense of peace and clarity through various techniques like focusing on the breath or repeating a mantra.

2. Mindfulness: Embracing the Present Moment

Mindfulness is about being present, paying non-judgmental attention to the current moment, and encompassing our thoughts, feelings, and bodily sensations. It's about becoming aware of our internal and external experiences without getting caught up. Practicing mindfulness can be as simple as savoring a mindful bite of food or taking a mindful walk, allowing us to appreciate the richness of the present.

3. Prayer: A Bridge to the Unseen

Prayer serves as a bridge between the visible and the unseen. It is a form of communication with a higher power, be it a deity, a universal force, or even our inner wisdom. Through prayer, we can express gratitude, seek guidance, offer confession, or simply connect in a spirit of reverence. This deeply personal and individual experience can nurture a sense of connection and belonging.

4. Yoga: A Union of Mind, Body, and Spirit

While often recognized for its physical postures, yoga encompasses a profound spiritual dimension. It aims to unite the mind, body, and spirit through a combination of physical postures (asanas), breathing exercises (pranayama), and meditation. Through this practice, we cultivate self-awareness, discipline, and a connection to a higher purpose.

5. The Resonant Chants of the Soul:

Chanting involves the repetitive recitation of sounds, mantras, or sacred texts. This practice can induce deep relaxation, focusing the mind and fostering a sense of connection. Imagine the rhythmic chanting creating a powerful wave of sound, washing away worries and uniting you with a sense of community or a higher power.

6. Delving Deep with Contemplation:

Contemplation invites you to focus your mind on a specific idea, question, or scripture, engaging in deep reflection and seeking a deeper understanding. It's like holding a precious jewel in the palm of your hand, turning it over and over again, exploring its facets to reveal hidden depths of meaning and wisdom. Through contemplation, you can gain valuable personal insights, experience spiritual growth, and discover a renewed sense of purpose and direction.

7. Serving with Compassion:

Acts of service, like volunteering or simply helping others in need, can be a powerful way to connect with something larger than ourselves and contribute to the greater good. By offering your time, skills, or resources, you cultivate compassion, humility, and a sense of purpose while fulfilling your spiritual need to connect and positively impact the world. Imagine the ripples of kindness spreading out from your actions, touching the lives of others, and creating a more harmonious and interconnected world.

The truest form of spiritual growth often lies not in reaching a destination but in the very act of journeying inwards. These are some of the many practices that help people heal themselves spiritually. Healing from trauma is a life-long journey, and every individual has their way of coping, but spirituality can be the ultimate source of healing from trauma and understanding it mindfully.

Spirituality and Trauma: A Path Towards Understanding and Transcendence

Trauma can shatter our sense of self, the world, and our place within it. Following this, spirituality can provide a framework for understanding and overcoming suffering and chaos. Trauma often challenges our fundamental beliefs about safety, justice, and the inherent goodness of the world. Through faith, connection to a higher power, or belief in an overarching purpose, spirituality can help re-establish meaning and order. It allows us to see our suffering not as random cruelty but as a part of a larger, potentially transformative journey.

Spiritual communities often provide a much-needed support system, offering compassion, understanding, and a sense of belonging during the isolating experience of trauma. Shared rituals and practices can help ground survivors, providing a sense of comfort and continuity amid personal upheaval.

Many spiritual traditions cultivate self-compassion and forgiveness, both towards oneself and others. These can be powerful tools in healing from trauma, helping survivors release self-blame, guilt, and the often-debilitating anger that can follow traumatic experiences.

Furthermore, Spirituality often nurtures hope, even in the darkest of times. It offers a belief in something larger than the suffering, suggesting the potential for growth, transformation, and a greater purpose beyond the pain. This hope can fuel resilience, allowing survivors to endure and transcend their traumatic experiences.

Techniques like meditation, prayer, and contemplation can offer concrete ways to calm the mind, connect with a sense of inner peace, and find solace in the face of trauma's lingering effects. They provide a safe space to process emotions, integrate experiences, and ultimately rebuild a sense of self.

It's vital to recognize that spirituality serves as a powerful complement, offering an additional dimension of healing and providing a unique framework for understanding the journey toward wholeness. Many people cure their trauma from spiritual practices and transform their lives completely. It is just one motivated step you have to take and then evolve as a healed and healthy person in this life.

From Darkness to Light - Hanah's Journey

Hanah was a successful corporate officer. Working day and night and chasing her dreams throughout her life. A few years back, Hanah had lost her way. Years of chasing material success had left her feeling empty and disconnected. Then, unfortunately, she faced a devastating loss – the death of her close friend that shattered her world, plunging her into deep despair. In her darkest moments, she tried yoga and began to explore its gentle movements and focused breathing tentatively. As her practice deepened, so did a newfound connection with her body and mind. Gradually, Hanah began to find a stillness within the chaos of her grief. She started to see that she was more than her pain and that life held greater meaning than she'd once believed.

Her spiritual awakening was not a single, dramatic moment but rather an unfolding shift in perspective – a realization that connectedness, compassion, and living in the present were her pathways to healing.

The Power of Surrender - Michael's Transformation

Michael was a self-proclaimed atheist, priding himself on his logic and reason. He believed life was a random series of events with no greater meaning. However, a series of unexpected challenges – health issues, financial struggles, and a strained relationship – crumbled his sense of control. Feeling desperate, he reluctantly agreed to attend a meditation retreat with his partner. Initially, he felt skeptical but reluctantly drawn into its practices. The silence, mindfulness, and focus on his breath began to chip away at his cynicism. One evening, during a guided meditation, he felt a profound sense of surrendering to a force larger than himself. This didn't mean he suddenly embraced a specific religion, but he did acknowledge a deeper dimension to life. From that moment, he began to rebuild, no longer fueled by ego but by a growing awareness of his connection to something bigger.

Each person's spiritual journey is unique. There's no single "right" way to experience an awakening or transformation. Many such experiences are gradual, not sudden, revelations. Spiritual awakenings don't always make life easy but may provide a framework of understanding within which to navigate challenges.

Using Spiritual Practices to Navigate Childhood Trauma

Childhood trauma can leave lasting scars on our emotional and spiritual well-being. While professional help is crucial, spiritual practices can offer valuable tools alongside therapy, providing a framework for understanding and navigating the healing journey. Here are some ways spiritual practices can help overcome childhood trauma:

Finding Meaning and Hope:

Trauma can shatter our sense of trust and purpose. Spiritual practices can offer a framework for meaning-making, connecting the experience to a larger narrative. This can be through faith in a higher power, belief in life's interconnectedness, or the human spirit's inherent resilience. Finding meaning helps us see beyond the immediate pain and cultivate hope for a brighter future.

Cultivating Self-Compassion and Forgiveness:

Trauma often leads to self-blame and guilt. Spiritual practices like meditation and mindfulness can help us develop self-compassion, allowing us to acknowledge and accept our experiences without judgment. Forgiveness, not necessarily of the perpetrator but of ourselves, can also be a powerful tool. It allows us to release the burden of negativity and move forward.

Building Inner Strength and Resilience:

Many spiritual practices, like yoga and martial arts, involve physical disciplines that can enhance our sense of inner strength and resilience. This also translates to emotional resilience, enabling us to manage difficult emotions better and cope with challenges.

Building Connection and Community:

Trauma can make us feel isolated and alone. Spiritual communities can provide a safe space for connection and belonging. Sharing experiences with others who understand can be incredibly validating and offer support and encouragement.

Finding Peace and Acceptance:

Many spiritual practices, like prayer and meditation, aim to cultivate inner peace and acceptance. These practices can help us find calm amidst the storm of emotions and allow us to accept what we cannot change.

Spiritual Practices to Consider:

- Meditation: Helps quiet the mind, process emotions, and cultivate self-awareness.

- Mindfulness: Allows us to be present with our experiences without judgment, promoting acceptance and emotional regulation.

- Prayer: Provides comfort, fosters connection to a higher power, and can be a source of strength and guidance.

- Yoga: Combines physical postures, breathing exercises, and meditation, promoting physical and mental well-being.

- Journaling: Allows for reflection, expressing emotions, and tracking progress on the healing journey.

There are many different ways through which people find healing through spirituality, like meditation, prayer, and sharing stories. These practices can help us understand and overcome difficult experiences, like when someone has been hurt or wronged in the past. Remember, everyone's journey is different. Therefore, no two people will be able to heal similarly. Try different things and see what helps you feel better and more connected to yourself and others.

Chapter 6: Self-Discovery

"The absence of self-love can never be replaced with the presence of people's love for you."

-Edmond Mbiaka

Self-love and self-compassion are fundamental pillars of well-being. While they go hand-in-hand, they each offer unique aspects. Self-love establishes the core belief that you are worthy of love and respect simply for who you are. And this isn't just about love from others; it involves pouring into your cup first with all the care and consideration you pour into others. It's about embracing your strengths and weaknesses, acknowledging your imperfections, and prioritizing your growth through self-care and personal development.

Self-compassion, on the other hand, translates this belief into action. It's basically the practice of treating yourself with the same kindness, understanding, and support you would extend to a close friend facing a similar challenge. This may include acknowledging your struggles and emotions without judgment, offering yourself forgiveness for mistakes, and viewing them as opportunities to learn and bounce back as a better version of yourself.

It is like treating yourself with the same unwavering support you offer a loved one. You surely wouldn't belittle them for their flaws or failures. Instead, you would rather offer encouragement and a helping hand. In simple terms, self-compassion is what demands the same nurturing and supportive attitude towards yourself, especially during difficult times.

However, building self-love and self-compassion is not as easy as it reads; it's a muscle that one must continually strengthen for a lifetime. It can be made possible by being self-aware, which is exploring your values, interests, and what brings you joy, ultimately leading you to establish a strong foundation. Setting healthy boundaries further allows you to prioritize your well-being by saying no to protect your time and energy. In addition, engaging in activities that nourish your physical and mental health, challenging negative self-talk with a more positive inner voice, and practicing self-forgiveness are all crucial aspects of this journey.

So, self-love and self-compassion are two closely linked concepts that work together to build a positive and healthy relationship with oneself. Self-love is the appreciation and regard we hold for ourselves, encompassing our strong and weak points and everything in between. It's about valuing ourselves as worthy of happiness and fulfillment. On the other hand, self-compassion emphasizes the gentle and supportive approach we take towards ourselves throughout our life journeys.

They work hand-in-hand because self-love provides the foundation for self-compassion; they both form a supportive cycle, reinforcing each other. We're more likely to respond to failures or shortcomings with understanding when we value ourselves. This self-compassion, in turn, allows us to face challenges constructively without resorting to harsh self-criticism. When we treat ourselves with kindness and understanding during harsh times, we cultivate a more resilient sense of self-love, creating a positive feedback loop supporting our growth and development. As self-love grows, we're better equipped to offer ourselves compassion, which strengthens our sense of self.

Facing and Embracing One's Own Vulnerabilities

Facing and embracing our vulnerabilities is an important step towards self-discovery, personal growth, and deeper connections with others. Vulnerability often carries a negative connotation associated with weakness or fragility. However, embracing vulnerability involves acknowledging our emotions, fears, and imperfections with honesty and self-acceptance, which isn't everybody's cup of tea, as it takes courage to show up unfiltered and then build genuine connections with those around us. It's basically about shedding the mask of perfection and allowing ourselves to be seen authentically. It takes more than you think to show up as that version of yourself in a world that might use your authenticity against you. But much to your surprise, it's just a game of finding the right balance and knowing when to and not be vulnerable.

However, to come off as your most authentic self, you must first know who you are at your core. This means that self-awareness requires self-discovery, and self-discovery requires self-reflection and self-honesty.

While it can be challenging, embracing vulnerability paradoxically fosters a sense of courage and authenticity, paving the way for genuine connections. When we share our vulnerabilities, we open ourselves up to the possibility of deeper intimacy and understanding in our relationships. It allows others to connect with us on a more human level and creates space for reciprocal vulnerability, further strengthening our bonds.

Furthermore, embracing vulnerability allows us to confront our fears and anxieties head-on. Once we learn the art of acknowledging our vulnerabilities, we can begin to address them and work towards overcoming them. This might involve seeking professional help, confiding in a trusted friend, or engaging in self-help practices. Doing this, as a result, promotes resilience and self-compassion as we learn to make our way through challenges with self-acceptance and a willingness to grow. So, facing and embracing vulnerabilities is not a sign of weakness but a demonstration of strength and courage, which paves the way for personal transformation and deeper connections.

The Role of Forgiveness in the Healing Journey

"Hurt people hurt people."

-Chip Dodd

Forgiveness plays a vital role in the healing journey, but it's important to understand it's not a one-time act or a condoning of wrongdoing. Instead, forgiveness is a process of letting go of anger, resentment, and negativity associated with a hurtful experience. It's about releasing these emotions' grip on us and choosing to move forward. Forgiveness doesn't erase the hurt or minimize what happened, but it allows us to break free from the cycle of pain and negativity that can hold us back.

This process can be challenging, especially for deep wounds. It may involve acknowledging the hurt we experienced, understanding the perpetrator's motivations (if possible), and practicing self-compassion throughout the journey. Forgiveness is in no way about reconciliation with the person who wronged us. In some cases, forgiveness might simply be about releasing the burden of resentment for our peace of mind. So, sometimes, forgiving the person who did you wrong can be for selfish reasons, and if doing that makes you feel better, then there is nothing wrong about doing so. And, of course, moving on with a clean and light heart has a ripple effect because, as they say, *"If you don't heal from what hurt you, you'll bleed on people who never cut you."*

In addition, the phrase "hurt people hurt people" suggests that individuals who have experienced emotional pain, trauma, or abuse are more likely to inflict pain on others themselves. The concept helps us understand how negative experiences can sometimes lead people to perpetuate those experiences in their interactions, creating a cycle of pain. It is not to say that everyone who experiences hurt goes on to inflict it on others. Many people forgive, heal, and choose healthier ways to cope; the good news is that you could be one of those people. And honestly, while someone's past experiences might explain their behavior, it doesn't excuse it. They are still responsible for their actions.

Thus, the benefits of forgiveness are significant. By letting go of negativity, we can experience reduced stress, improved mental health, and inner peace. Forgiveness also allows us to invest our emotional energy into positive experiences and relationships and grow toward something meaningful rather than dwelling on the past and something that can't be changed. On the contrary, like a bundle of love and compassion, healed people can help heal others. This means that those who have overcome their pain can help others heal from theirs, those who prioritize their own mental and emotional health can create a positive and supportive environment for others to thrive, and when people feel empowered to overcome challenges and live fulfilling lives, they can inspire and support others to do the same.

However, it's important to remember that forgiveness is a personal journey, and there's no right or wrong way to do it. We all move at a different pace, so be patient with yourself and take the time you need to process your emotions and reach a place of forgiveness.

How Forgiveness Will Help You Recover from Childhood Trauma

Childhood trauma can leave deep scars, but forgiveness can be a powerful tool on the road to healing. It's important to remember that forgiveness isn't about pretending the trauma didn't happen or forgetting the pain it caused. Instead, it's about letting go of the resentment and anger that can hold you back from moving forward and your first step toward breaking the so-called 'generational curse.'

The first step is acknowledging and validating your emotions. Allow yourself to feel the anger, hurt, and sadness that come with your experience because suppressing these emotions can and will only hinder your healing process. Once you've acknowledged your feelings, try to see the situation differently. This doesn't mean excusing the perpetrator's actions, but it can help you move past blame and understand the situation in a new light.

After acknowledging what happened to you, focus on self-compassion instead of seeing yourself as a victim. Though you can be understanding towards the perpetrator's action, remember that you were still a child who deserved love and support.[13] So, be kind to yourself throughout this process. Healing from childhood trauma is a journey that takes time; it isn't linear, and there's no perfect way to do it. Be patient with yourself and celebrate your progress along the way.

There are also resources available to help you on your healing journey. Talking to a therapist can also provide support and guidance as you process your trauma and work towards forgiveness. Connecting with others who have experienced similar trauma through support groups can also be validating and helpful. Don't forget to practice self-care by taking care of your physical and mental health through healthy eating, exercise, and relaxation techniques.

---

[13]https://dergipark.org.tr/en/download/article-file/2589833#:~:text=In%20the%20process%20of%20helping,successful%20in%20forgiving%20the%20situation.

Chapter 7: Relationships and Healing

"We're often afraid of being vulnerable, but vulnerability creates genuine connection."

-Gabby Bernstein

People who have only experienced toxic relationships may generally have a warped view of what love and connection are truly about. They might be skeptical of everyone's intentions and find it difficult to trust and open up due to constant negativity. Healthy dynamics like boundaries, open communication, and interdependence can be entirely misunderstood. They might confuse healthy boundaries with coldness, open communication with criticism, and interdependence with codependency, making it challenging to recognize or build healthy relationships for themselves.

Furthermore, the fear of vulnerability is often ingrained in those who've been hurt by manipulation and control. As a result, the fear can make them hesitant to express their true selves or be open for fear of getting hurt again. So, the question is: *how would a healthy relationship feel to them?*

Well, think about a dynamic that initially feels unfamiliar and even uncomfortable. The give-and-take, mutual respect, and open communication that are hallmarks of a healthy relationship can be a big adjustment from what they're used to. They might be suspicious of a partner's kindness or support, wondering what the catch is, or waiting for the other shoe to drop. Even healthy boundaries and independence within a relationship can be confusing or feel wrong. It sounds sad, but they might even experience guilt for prioritizing their own needs and interests.

The good news is this cycle can be broken. Therapy can be a powerful tool to help them understand healthy relationship dynamics, develop trust, and build communication skills. Here are some signs that a relationship might be healthier than they're used to: feeling safe and respected, having a partner who encourages their dreams and celebrates their successes, and being able to disagree without resorting to insults or blame but instead focusing on finding solutions together. It can be a journey, but with time and effort, someone who has only experienced toxic relationships can learn to build healthy and fulfilling connections.[14]

What Does a Healthy Relationship Look Like?

In essence, healthy relationships, whether romantic, platonic, or familial, depend on a strong foundation of mutual respect, trust, and support, and these core elements act as the building blocks for a thriving connection.

For once, think about a relationship where you can be completely honest and open with your partner, knowing they'll listen without judgment. You feel safe expressing your opinions and feelings because they value them, and the open communication extends to positive and negative emotions, all delivered respectfully.

---

[14]https://medium.com/curious/subtle-ways-your-childhood-could-poison-a-healthy-relationship-
16e0127b7083#:~:text=A%20healthy%20relationship%20can%20give,poison%20that%2
0deteriorates%20its%20health.

Healthy relationships also involve a delicate balance of interdependence. You rely on each other for support but also maintain your individuality and interests. Your happiness shouldn't hinge solely on your partner. Likewise, healthy boundaries are also profound because these boundaries establish respect for each other's personal space and privacy. Both partners feel comfortable saying no and confident that their boundaries *will be* respected. Similar values and beliefs also play a significant role. While you won't agree on everything, there should be a sense of compatibility in your outlooks on life and mutual respect for each other's differences, as these shared values create a strong foundation for the relationship.

Furthermore, healthy relationships encourage personal growth and ambitions in both partners. You celebrate each other's successes and offer unwavering support during challenges. Undoubtedly, disagreements are inevitable, but healthy couples can work through them constructively because the focus is on finding solutions rather than placing blame.

And lastly, fairness and balance are equally essential. Ideally, both partners contribute fairly to household chores, decision-making, and emotional support. Remember, healthy relationships take work and effort from both sides. And whenever you feel unsure about the health of your relationships, it is recommended to seek guidance from a therapist or counselor.

Nurturing Healthy Relationships

Have you ever wondered what nurturing healthy relationships is like? Well, it is like tending to a beautiful garden. It requires consistent care and attention, but the rewards are abundant. These relationships blossom into sources of support and healing, offering a safe haven for you to grow and thrive.

As discussed, mutual respect and trust build the foundation of any healthy relationship. This means feeling comfortable being authentic and knowing your partner values your opinions and feelings. Open communication flourishes in this environment and allows you to freely express your joys and challenges without fear of judgment or hiding behind any façade; you just know you can be your truest self around this person.

Healthy relationships also provide a strong support network. Your partner becomes your cheerleader, who celebrates your successes and offers unwavering encouragement during both good and tough times. Knowing you have someone who believes in you and your dreams can be a powerful source of strength, especially when facing life's unavoidable challenges.

People who have only been in toxic relationships and feel an excessive need for another person's acceptance, approval, and validation do not quite realize this, but healthy boundaries are essential for nurturing relationships. In fact, they should be a non-negotiable to ensure your own and your relationship's well-being. Boundaries are healthy because they mark where your partner ends and where you and your overall well-being begin. They establish a sense of personal space and respect for each other's needs. Knowing your boundaries are respected allows you to be more present and engaged in the relationship, making it long-lasting.

Effective communication is another key ingredient. This involves actively listening to your partner and expressing yourself clearly. It also means navigating disagreements constructively and focusing on finding solutions together rather than avoiding accountability. Not just that, nurturing healthy relationships also allows for emotional intimacy. You feel safe sharing your vulnerabilities and expressing your true self. Due to this emotional connection, both individuals feel a sense of belonging and strengthen their bond.

So, by nurturing these qualities within your relationships, you cultivate a safe space for healing and growth. The support and encouragement you receive can help you deal with life's challenges, build resilience, and experience a greater well-being. In the end, healthy relationships are a two-way street. Investing time and effort into nurturing them will benefit you and your partner and create a source of strength and joy in your life.

Challenges in Love and Communication Due to Childhood Trauma

But unfortunately, childhood trauma can leave a lasting impact, affecting how you experience love and communication in your adult relationships. Here's a closer look at some of the challenges you might face:

Love and Trust Can Be Difficult

Trauma can make it difficult to open yourself up to love and trust. You might fear getting hurt again, subconsciously pushing potential partners away to avoid intimacy. Sharing your true self with someone can also feel risky, which can hinder the development of deep emotional connections. Early experiences can also shape your perception of relationships. If you witnessed unhealthy dynamics as a child, you might unconsciously recreate them in your relationships with partners.

Communication Can Be a Struggle

Trauma can make it difficult to manage your emotions effectively. You might struggle to express your feelings in a healthy way, leading to emotional outbursts or withdrawal. If you experienced negative communication patterns as a child, you might also misinterpret your partner's words or actions, potentially leading to misunderstandings and conflict. Resolving disagreements constructively can also be a challenge. You might resort to unhealthy coping mechanisms like shutting down or blaming your partner, which is why healing is much needed before diving into any relationship and committing to another individual.

Additional Challenges to Relationships

Childhood trauma can also affect your relationships in other ways. Low self-esteem, a common result of trauma, can make it difficult to believe you deserve love and respect. This can manifest as jealousy, possessiveness, or difficulty setting boundaries in your relationships. You might also experience hypervigilance, constantly on guard for signs of rejection or betrayal, which can create anxiety and strain the relationship.

The good news is that healing is possible. There are resources available to help you overcome the challenges of childhood trauma and build fulfilling relationships. Therapy can be a powerful tool, helping you process your trauma, develop healthy coping mechanisms, and build stronger relationship skills. Connecting with others who have experienced similar challenges through support groups can also be validating and helpful. Prioritizing your physical and mental health through self-care practices like healthy eating, exercise, and relaxation techniques can also help you manage the effects of trauma. So, by seeking help and working on healing, you can build the strong and healthy relationships you deserve.

How Healthy Relationships Can Help You Recover from Your Childhood Trauma

Did you know that, on the flip side, healthy relationships can turn out to be a powerful force for healing after childhood trauma? Let us discuss why:

Safe Space and Support: A healthy relationship provides a safe and supportive environment where you can begin to heal. Knowing you have someone who believes in you and cares for you unconditionally can be incredibly comforting, and this sense of security allows you to feel more open to processing your trauma and working through difficult emotions.

Validation and Understanding: In a healthy relationship, your partner validates your experiences and feelings. They understand that your past trauma may impact you in the present, and they offer support without judgment. The validation you receive from their end can be incredibly healing, finally allowing you to feel heard and understood.

Improved Self-Esteem: Such relationships can help you rebuild your self-esteem, which is often damaged by childhood trauma. A partner who appreciates and respects you can help you challenge negative self-beliefs and start seeing yourself more positively.

Healthy Communication Skills: Positive relationships involve clear and open communication. By practicing healthy communication with your partner, you can slowly learn to constructively express your needs and feelings. It can be especially helpful if you struggled with communication as a child.

Positive Relationship Models: If you didn't experience healthy bonds in your childhood, being in a healthy relationship now can provide a positive model for future connections. You can learn what healthy relationships look and feel like and how to build them in other areas.

Increased Resilience: These kinds of relationships can additionally make you more resilient because knowing you have someone to rely on can give you the strength to face challenges and setbacks related to your trauma. Your partner can be a source of encouragement and motivation as you work on healing.

In addition to this, while trauma can lead to feelings of isolation, a healthy relationship can help you combat loneliness and feel more connected to others. Plus, feeling like you belong and are loved can be a powerful antidote to the feelings of isolation and worthlessness that often accompany trauma. And it doesn't end there. Healthy relationships can be a source of stress relief. When you spend time with someone you care about, you experience a certain drop in your stress levels and improved overall well-being.

Having said that, it's important to remember that while healthy relationships can be powerful in healing your trauma, it's important to seek professional help if you're struggling to cope with childhood trauma and not solely rely on your loved ones to heal you. You must take the matter into your own hands and consciously try to heal yourself to make space for and nurture healthy and non-toxic relationships in your life because you deserve them.

It cannot be stressed enough, but consider seeking a therapist as they are there to help you, and it's always great to have an unbiased perspective on your problems and solutions offered to process and heal from the wounds you never deserved to have as a child. They can provide additional support and guidance as you work towards healing.

Chapter 8: Practical Tips

Like any skill we want to develop, our healing journey benefits greatly from consistent practice, and there are several reasons why this is the case.

Firstly, practice allows for improvement and refinement. Similar to how we improve physical or mental abilities, the tools we use for healing require repetition to become more effective. Whether it's managing stress through meditation or developing healthier communication patterns, practicing allows us to improve at these techniques and identify areas where we can improve further.

Healing often involves establishing new behaviors and routines that support our well-being. Through consistent practice, these behaviors become ingrained habits, and it becomes easier to integrate them seamlessly into our daily lives. Long-term beneficial change is made possible by this constancy.

Interestingly, research shows that practice can literally change our brains. The more we rehearse a specific activity, the stronger the neural connections associated with it become, and this translates to these activities becoming more automatic and easier to perform over time. In the context of healing, this can mean strengthening positive coping mechanisms or emotional regulation techniques and making them readily available when needed.

Also, the healing journey is rarely smooth because setbacks are unavoidable. However, consistent practice allows us to develop resilience. When we regularly engage in our healing practices, we build the strength and flexibility to bounce back from challenges and keep moving forward on our path to well-being.

So, conclusively, while consistent practice may not always be easy, it is the key to unlocking the full potential of our healing journey, and by dedicating ourselves to practicing the tools and techniques that support our well-being, we can create lasting positive change in our lives.

Love and Spirituality

Love and spirituality are two cornerstones of human experience, profoundly impacting our daily lives and sense of well-being.

Love, in all its forms, transcends romantic relationships. It encompasses our deep affection for family and friends, our connection with nature, and even the joy we derive from cherished activities. At its core, love cultivates kindness, compassion, empathy, and the power of forgiveness. It promotes a sense of connection and belonging, reminding us that we are not alone in this vast world. On the other hand, self-love is the bedrock upon which all other forms of love flourish. Accepting and appreciating ourselves makes us better prepared to give and receive love in our relationships.

On the other hand, spirituality is about forging a connection with something larger than ourselves. This connection can take various forms, be it a deep appreciation for nature, a belief in a higher power, or a pursuit of a meaningful purpose in life. Spiritual activities that promote peace and clarity, as well as a deep sense of inner calm, include meditation, prayer, and just being in nature. They can also provide direction and meaning and guide us through life's challenges with greater resilience and a more positive outlook.

The beauty lies in how love and spirituality intertwine, as studies have shown that love and spirituality can have a calming effect. Many spiritual traditions emphasize the importance of loving-kindness and compassion, qualities that mirror the essence of love itself. Feeling connected to something larger than ourselves can make us more open to giving and receiving love from others. Ultimately, love and spirituality are powerful tools that help us navigate life's complexities with greater strength and a more hopeful perspective.

Ultimately, there's no single path to experiencing love and spirituality. The key is to find practices and beliefs that resonate with you and enrich your daily life with meaning and joy.

Practical Exercises and Rituals for Integrating Love and Spirituality into Daily Life

Weaving love and spirituality into your daily life can significantly enhance your experience. Here are some practical exercises and rituals to get you started:

Nurturing Love:

- Cultivate gratitude by starting or ending your day with a simple practice. Take a few minutes to reflect on three things you're grateful for, big or small, because appreciating life's blessings strengthens feelings of love and abundance.

• Spread kindness by brightening someone's day with random acts. You can do this by holding the door open for a stranger, offering a genuine compliment, or simply lending a helping hand. The thing is that these small gestures spread positivity and remind you of the joy of giving.

• Practice loving-kindness meditation, which is powerful for cultivating love. Guided meditations are readily available online or in apps, and one can begin by directing loving thoughts towards yourself. Gradually extend this love to loved ones, acquaintances, and even those you find challenging.

• Deepen connections with loved ones by dedicating quality time to interact with them. Share a meal, have a heartfelt phone call, or simply hold hands while watching TV, as prioritizing these connections strengthens the bonds of love in your life.

Embracing Spirituality:

• Practice mindfulness throughout the day by taking a few mindful breaths and focusing on the sensation of your breath entering and leaving your nostrils. This simple act anchors you in the present moment and fosters inner peace.

• Connect with nature by immersing yourself in it, even if it's just for a few minutes on your balcony or in a nearby park. Spending time in nature provides a sense of linking to something larger and beyond yourself.

• Create a sacred space by dedicating a corner of your room or a specific object for your spiritual practice. This could be a place for meditation, prayer, or quiet reflection. This is because having a designated space fosters reverence and routine in your spiritual journey.

- Express gratitude in writing by maintaining a gratitude journal and consciously make it a habit to practice thankfulness for the blessings in your life, big or small. Reviewing this journal can be a powerful reminder of your abundance and cultivate a sense of contentment.

Weaving Love and Spirituality Together

Weaving love and spirituality together can be achieved through your daily actions. Speak with kindness by being mindful of your words towards yourself and others, and let your speech be filled with compassion and understanding. As a result, this loving communication builds positive connections with those around you and strengthens your own spirit.

Engage in sacred service by combining love and service and volunteer for a cause you care about. Helping others in need connects you to your spiritual core and develops community. It also allows you to express love through action and not just words.

Finally, practice mindful movement by integrating mindfulness into your physical activity. Whether it's yoga, dance, or a brisk walk, focus on your body's sensations as you move. This practice combines physical well-being with present-moment awareness and fully lets you present in your body and spirit.

Remember that consistency is key. So, start small and gradually incorporate these practices into your daily life. You'll be amazed at how even small acts of love and spiritual connection can significantly enhance the quality of your life.

Mind and Body Practices to Ground and Centre Yourself

Are you feeling overwhelmed by daily stress or emotions? Sometimes, the best remedy is simply returning to the present moment and reconnecting with yourself. Here are some effective mind and body practices for grounding and centering that can help you achieve this inner peace and stability whenever needed. These techniques are easy to learn and integrate into your daily routine, allowing you to manage stress more effectively and cultivate a sense of calm.

Focus on Your Breath

- **Simple Breathwork:** This is a foundational practice for grounding and centering. Find a comfortable seated or lying down position and close your eyes or soften your gaze. Then, take slow, deep breaths through your nose and feel your belly rise and fall with each inhalation and exhalation. Next, count silently to four on the inhale and six on the exhale, or simply focus on the natural rhythm of your breath. Practice this for a few minutes, letting your mind quiet and your body relax.

- **Alternate Nostril Breathing (Nadi Shodhana):** This technique helps balance the nervous system and promote calmness. Begin by sitting comfortably with your spine erect, and then close your right nostril with your thumb and inhale slowly through your left nostril. Hold your breath for a comfortable count (avoid straining), then close your left nostril with your ring finger. Exhale slowly through your right nostril. Repeat by inhaling through the right nostril, holding, and then exhaling through the left nostril. In this practice, you'll be required to continue alternating nostrils for several minutes.

Body Scan Meditation

Lie down comfortably on your back or sit in a chair with your feet flat on the floor and soften your gaze; you can even close your eyes. Bring your attention to your toes and wiggle them gently. Try to notice any sensations in your feet, such as tingling, warmth, or coolness. Slowly scan your body upwards and notice any tension or tightness in your calves, knees, thighs, etc. Acknowledge the sensations without judgment and continue to scan your body, moving up to your torso, arms, head, and neck. When you finish the scan, take a few deep breaths and gently wiggle your fingers and toes.

Progressive Muscle Relaxation (PMR)

Progressive Muscle Relaxation is a technique that helps to release physical tension and promote relaxation. First and foremost, sit or lie down comfortably, tensing and relaxing different muscle groups in your body one at a time. For example, clench your fists tightly for a few seconds, then release and feel the tension melt away. Tense and relax your shoulders, arms, legs, face, and any other areas that hold tension. As you release each muscle group, focus on the feeling of relaxation spreading throughout your body.

Mindfulness Through the Senses

You can ground yourself in the present moment by focusing on your senses. Take a few minutes to observe the sights, sounds, smells, tastes, and textures around you. Notice the details: the color of the sky, the chirping of birds, the scent of a flower, the taste of your tea, and the texture of your clothing against your skin. By engaging your senses, you bring your awareness to the present moment and promote a sense of calmness.

Spending Time in Nature

Being in nature has a powerful grounding effect, and immersing yourself in nature helps quiet your mind and connect you to something bigger and beyond you. Walking in the park, sitting by a stream, or simply gazing at the trees. You can center yourself by noticing the feeling of the sun on your skin, the coolness of the breeze, and the sound of leaves rustling in the wind.

Making these techniques a regular part of your routine is key to building your ability to ground and center yourself whenever you feel off-balance. With consistent practice, you'll effectively develop the skills to manage stress and cultivate inner peace.

Crafting Your Personalized Healing Toolkit

The thing is that you're not alone if you're struggling with emotions and stress management. We all experience moments where we need to find our center and promote inner peace. The good news is that you have the power to create a personalized healing toolkit filled with practices and techniques that resonate with you. The toolkit will be your go-to resource for grounding yourself, managing stress, and nurturing emotional well-being. Here's how to get started:

1. Identify Your Needs:

The first step is self-awareness. Reflect on the emotions that typically throw you off balance. Is it stress? Anxiety? Anger? Do you struggle with low mood or difficulty focusing? Once you understand your emotional triggers, you can choose tools that effectively address those needs.

2. Explore Different Techniques:

The world of self-care offers a vast array of practices. Experiment with different techniques to see what resonates with you. This section from the previous prompt offered some grounding and centering practices like breathwork, meditation, and mindful movement. You can explore journaling, art therapy, spending time in nature, listening to calming music, or spending time with loved ones.

3. Curate Your Toolkit:

Based on your needs and preferences, curate your personal toolkit and include practices that address both immediate needs (like calming techniques for anxiety) and long-term well-being (like mindfulness meditation for overall emotional regulation). And don't overload yourself; choose a manageable number of practices you can integrate into your daily or weekly routine.

4. Make it Accessible:

Keep your toolkit readily available. Write down your chosen practices on notecards and place them around your workspace or home. Maybe download guided meditations or relaxation apps on your phone because having easy access reminds you to utilize your toolkit when needed.

5. Personalize and Refine:

Your toolkit is a dynamic entity, not a static collection, and as your needs evolve, so should your toolkit. Experiment with new techniques, discard practices that no longer serve you, and regularly evaluate and refine your toolkit to ensure it continues to meet your evolving needs.

Most people don't understand that self-care is not a luxury but a necessity. Investing time and effort in creating your personalized healing toolkit empowers you to face life's challenges with greater resilience and innate contentment.

To sum up, our well-being thrives on consistent practices like meditation and spending time in nature. These practices help us manage stress, develop emotional resilience, and strengthen our connection to ourselves and the world around us. By doing the bare minimum for ourselves, which is creating a personalized healing toolkit filled with practices that resonate with us, we can raise our inner peace and have a more positive outlook on life.

Chapter 9: Common Roadblocks

We all know that life's favorite hobby is throwing us curveballs, especially when we wish not to receive them. We face hardships, setbacks, and adversity; during these times, two crucial qualities come into play: resilience and perseverance. These qualities work together to help us navigate challenges and emerge stronger and better on the other side of the mountain of problems and hardships.

Resilience is the mental and emotional strength that allows us to bounce back from difficult situations. Imagine a rubber band— yes, it can be stretched and pulled but returns to its original shape. A resilient person is like that rubber band, able to bend and flex without breaking. So, when faced with challenges, resilience is what allows us to adapt, find new solutions, and move forward.

On the other hand, perseverance is actually one's firm commitment to keep going even when faced with obstacles. It's the dedication and grit you need to pursue your goals and overcome challenges, no matter how long it takes. How climbing a mountain is tough, but with perseverance, the mountain climber keeps putting one foot in front of the other until they reach the summit. Perseverance is the quality of staying focused on our goals and pushing through moments of doubt or difficulty.

These qualities are important because life is full of ups and downs, and having both resilience and perseverance equips us to face these challenges head-on and reap a multitude of benefits. We experience increased mental and emotional well-being by bouncing back from setbacks, leading to less stress, anxiety, and depression. Perseverance allows us to achieve our goals; it helps us adopt a greater sense of accomplishment and boosts our confidence. As we face challenges repeatedly, we develop better strategies for overcoming obstacles and improving our problem-solving skills. Perseverance also strengthens our relationships by demonstrating commitment and dedication to those around us. Ultimately, overcoming challenges through resilience and perseverance cultivates self-awareness and permits us to learn from our experiences, finally leading us to personal growth.

The Roadblocks on the Path to Healing

The journey towards healing from childhood trauma is a process of self-discovery and growth. While filled with immense potential, it's natural to encounter roadblocks along the way. Let us shed light on some common challenges you might face:

First and foremost, the wounds of childhood trauma can leave lasting scars on your self-esteem. You might struggle with feelings of worthlessness, believing you don't deserve happiness or healing, and this negative self-talk can be a significant obstacle to progress. It can be a constant critic that chips away at your confidence and makes it difficult to believe in your ability to heal.

The memories associated with childhood trauma can be harrowing. You might experience fear, shame, or anger when revisiting the past. This can make it difficult to delve into the root causes of your struggles. Plus, facing all those harsh memories can be overwhelming and be yet another roadblock on your path, but avoiding them can hinder your healing, which is something you don't want.

Healing requires change, and change can be scary. You might find yourself clinging to familiar patterns, even if they're unhealthy, simply because you feel safe. Stepping outside your comfort zone can also be challenging, as it can mean letting go of old habits and behaviors that no longer serve you and venturing into the unknown.

But the catch is that healing isn't a linear process. There will be setbacks and moments where you regress; there will definitely be days when you'll feel you're not healing at all despite all your efforts. This can be discouraging, but it's important to remember that setbacks are a normal part of the journey. Don't let them define you. Instead, learn from them and keep moving forward. See setbacks as opportunities to refine your approach and build resilience.

Expecting instant results can lead to frustration and discouragement, as healing takes time and consistent effort. It's important to be patient with yourself and celebrate small victories along the way. Instead of focusing on how much more is left, for once, reflect on how far you've come and the progress you've made, no matter how small it seems. In the end, every step forward is a step closer to healing.

Healing sounds promising, but it can be a lonely journey, especially if you feel isolated from friends and family who don't understand your experiences. A lack of support can make staying motivated and persevering through challenges difficult. Thus, building a support system of people who can offer encouragement, understanding, and a safe space for you to express yourself is crucial.

Forgiveness, especially for those who inflicted the trauma, can be incredibly tough; however, holding onto anger and resentment only hinders your healing and is much more difficult. Finding a way to let go, even if it's just for yourself, is an important step in the healing process. Forgiveness doesn't mean condoning the perpetrator's actions but rather releasing yourself from the burden of negativity.

Despite these challenges, remember that healing is possible. With self-compassion, perseverance, and the right support system, you can overcome these roadblocks and build a better future for yourself.

Navigating Setbacks and Relapses on Your Healing Journey

The road to healing from childhood trauma is long and winding. There will be moments when you stumble, experience setbacks, or even find yourself slipping back into old patterns. But you must remember that this is a normal part of the process. The key is to have strategies in place to pick yourself up, learn from the experience, and keep moving forward on your path to healing.

Self-Compassion is Key:

First and foremost, you need to learn to be kind to yourself. Instead of wasting energy on self-criticism, acknowledge the effort you've already invested in your healing journey, embrace self-compassion, and remember that everyone experiences setbacks.

Identify Your Triggers:

Take some time to reflect on what led to the setback. Was it a particularly stressful situation? Certain emotions? Identifying your triggers can give you the space to develop strategies for avoiding them in the future. By understanding your triggers, you can proactively manage your responses.

Reconnect with Your Goals:

Remind yourself of the reasons you embarked on this journey of healing. Reconnect with the positive changes you're striving for, and very often, ask yourself about the kind of life you want to build for yourself. Reflecting on your goals can reignite your motivation and keep you focused on the bigger picture.

Don't Isolate Yourself:

Healing can be lonely, but you don't have to do it alone. Reach out for support from a trusted friend, therapist, or support group member. Sharing your struggles with others who understand can offer valuable encouragement and guidance, and talking about your experiences can be cathartic and help you process your emotions.

Prioritize Self-Care:

Make self-care a non-negotiable part of your life and prioritize activities that nourish your mind, body, and spirit. This might include exercise, meditation, spending time in nature, or engaging in hobbies you enjoy. Self-care strengthens your resilience and equips you to cope with challenges healthily.

Reframe Your Perspective:

Instead of seeing setbacks as failures, view them as opportunities for growth and learning. Analyze what went wrong, adjust your approach if needed, and use this experience to build your strength. Setbacks are not the end of the road; they are stepping stones on your path to healing.

Focus on Progress, Not Perfection:

As healing is not linear, you can expect ups and downs along the way. But even amidst that, rejoice in your small victories and acknowledge your progress, no matter how insignificant it may seem to you. Every step forward in the right direction is still a step closer.

Develop Healthy Coping Mechanisms:

Having healthy coping mechanisms allows you to constructively manage stress and difficult emotions. You can identify your very own healthy coping mechanisms that you can turn to during difficult times. This could include deep breathing exercises, journaling your thoughts and feelings, spending time with loved ones, or engaging in relaxation techniques like yoga or meditation.

Maintain a Growth Mindset:

Believe in your ability to learn and grow from your experiences because obstructions don't define you *at all*. They are part of the healing journey. So, maintain a growth mindset and trust you have the strength and resilience to overcome challenges.

Seek Professional Help:

If you're struggling to cope with setbacks on your own, consider seeking professional help from a therapist or counselor who specializes in trauma recovery. They can provide valuable tools, support, and guidance to help you deal with healing challenges and stay on track toward your goals.

Roadblocks are temporary and can be dealt with through self-empathy, determination, and the right support system.

The Case of Fetishization

Nowadays, the concept of healing from your trauma has quite literally been fetishized on the internet. Social media can portray healing as a trendy image—perfectly curated photos of yoga poses or meditation sessions, which overshadow the real struggles and challenges involved in the healing process, making it seem like a quick fix.

Sometimes, the focus is on outward appearances of healing (glowing skin, trendy practices) rather than the deeper emotional and psychological work it entails. Plus, the narrative of "just heal" or "good vibes only" can be insensitive to the complexities of trauma and the time it takes to heal. However, the key is to approach healing with a critical eye. To heal means to give yourself time to do the much-needed deep inner work. What works for one person might not work for another, so one must find what resonates with them and be discerning of the healing resources they choose for themselves.

Though the focus on healing can be a positive sign, reflects a growing awareness of mental health and well-being, and encourages people to prioritize self-care and seek help when needed, the concept shouldn't be fetishized. Healing is a deeply personal process, and its true value lies not in attaining some trendy image of well-being but in the profound transformation it can bring about in your life.

By approaching healing with authenticity and a commitment to self-discovery, you can unearth inner strength, cultivate healthier relationships, and build a stronger and fulfilling sense of self. The focus should be on the quality of the journey, the personal growth it promotes, and its positive impact on your life, not on checking off boxes or following a prescriptive path.

Chapter 10: Conclusion

We've reached the end of the book, and on this journey together, you've likely discovered the core message that love and spirituality can heal one from childhood trauma.

Well, the central message of this book is that within us all lies the potential for profound healing and transformation, which is fueled by the power of love and guided by the wisdom of spiritual practices.

Our journey began with understanding trauma. We first explored the different types of traumas, with a particular focus on the dangers of childhood trauma, and dived deeper into the causes and lasting effects that childhood trauma can have on the mind, body, and spirit. The chapter also explored common coping mechanisms used to manage trauma while acknowledging their limitations.

Next, we shifted our focus to love and spirituality. We unpacked the concept of love in various forms, including self-love, romantic, and platonic love. That exploration was followed by a deep dive into spirituality and its role in healing. We highlighted the symbiotic relationship between love and spiritual practices and emphasized how they can work together to promote healing.

Love's power as a healing force was then examined through a scientific and psychological lens. In addition, real-life stories and case studies served as powerful examples of how love, emphasizing empathy, compassion, and connection, can be a developmental tool, particularly for those healing from childhood trauma.

Spiritual practices such as meditation, mindfulness, and prayer were then introduced as pathways to healing, and together, we learned how these practices provide support for understanding and transcending trauma. Stories of spiritual transformation were shared, along with how these practices can be used to overcome the effects of childhood trauma.

In addition, self-discovery emerged as a crucial healing element in a subsequent chapter. We discussed the importance of cultivating love and compassion for oneself. Facing and embracing one's vulnerabilities was highlighted, alongside the role of forgiveness in the healing journey. The chapter stressed the significance of forgiveness in recovering from childhood trauma. Plus, we understood healthy relationships as a source of support and healing and discussed how childhood trauma can create challenges in love and communication in our adulthood. However, the chapter also emphasized how healthy relationships can be vital to recovery. Not just that, we also presented tools and strategies to help you navigate your healing journey. All these chapters worked together to provide the foundation for the practical aspects of the book.

Radical Forgiveness and The Intersection of Self-Love and Shadow Work

Traditional forgiveness is often focused on letting go of resentment towards others who have wronged us. However, in the context of self-love and spiritual healing, a concept called "radical forgiveness" takes it a step further. It's about extending forgiveness not just to others but also to ourselves.

Here's why this is important: Trauma can often lead to self-blame, shame, and a critical inner voice. This negativity becomes a barrier to healing and self-love. Radical forgiveness allows us to acknowledge the pain we've experienced without judgment. We can accept that mistakes were made by ourselves or others and choose to release the negativity associated with those experiences.

This doesn't mean condoning the actions that caused the trauma. It's about understanding that everyone makes mistakes and that past experiences don't define who we are now. By releasing the burden of self-blame and negativity, we create space for self-compassion and acceptance, which opens the door to genuine self-love and allows us to move forward with a lighter heart.

Additionally, many spiritual traditions talk about the "shadow self," which is the unconscious aspects of our personality that hold negative emotions, limiting beliefs, and repressed desires. While these aspects can be scary to confront, shadow work, a practice of exploring and integrating our shadow self, can be a powerful tool for healing and self-love.

The connection is that often, the shadow self contains aspects of ourselves we learned to reject or suppress to cope with trauma. With this, we mean that by neglecting the shadow, we deny a part of who we are, which can deter our growth and the ability to love ourselves. Through self-love, we cultivate the courage to face the shadow self without judgment. We can explore these repressed aspects with empathy and understanding and integrate them into our whole selves.

This integration allows us to embrace all parts of ourselves, both the light and the dark, which nurtures wholeness and authenticity, leading to a more profound and genuine form of self-love.

These are just two lesser-known aspects of self-love and spiritual healing. The journey is unique for everyone, and the most important aspect is finding practices that sit well with you.

Now, armed with the knowledge gained from this guide, you are invited to embark on your own transformative journey. Embrace the power of love in all its forms—self-love, compassion, and connection with others. Study the wisdom of spiritual practices and allow them to guide you toward healing and inner peace. The path may not always be easy, but self-love and spiritual growth rewards are immeasurable. Take that first step because you deserve healing and a life filled with love and light.